The Memory of Her

poems by

Matt Amott

First edition. Printed in the USA.

ISBN: 978-1-926860-67-1

Some of these poems appeared in various forms in the following publications: *The Coast Is Clear*: Six Ft. Swells Press, *Get Well Soon*: Epic Rites Press, The Poeming Pigeon: The Poetry Box, In Between Hangovers, and Midnight Lane Boutique.

Epic Rites Press publications are distributed worldwide by Tree Killer Ink. For more information about *The Memory of Her* (and other books and publications from Epic Rites Press) please visit the Epic Rites website at www.epicrites.org.

Epic Rites: any press is only as "small" as its thinking

Contents

Postcards and Poetry

The best poets can capture a moment in time and write a poem around them. If they are really good, they can make a book out of these moments and if they are truly talented then they make us want to read the book again and again. This is the case with Matt Amott's *The Memory of Her.* These poems are sincere and simple. They evoke the same feeling as reading a postcard or slowly flipping through an old photo album. These are poems of bars, bikinis, backpacking, break-ups, best friends, and beauty. Of seasons and search for companionship, speedy getaways and summer crushes, whiskey shots and twelve hour shifts. Memories we cannot forget.

It is refreshing to read a poet who doesn't want to confuse, condescend, lecture or pontificate through poetry. Poems that are not written for nominations or awards — but for the heart. This collection is meant to be read, passed around, talked about and sent to your best friends; to be shared. Matt strives to be nothing more than clear and honest with the reader. He sips his drink slowly and appreciates the moment; before, during and in the aftermath. This is the gift of a good poet.

Matt's poems in *The Memory of Her* bring to life the simple pleasures and slight pains that life and poetry present us.

These are memories you will not forget,

Todd Cirillo, poet, editor
11:59 pm
12/21/18

The Memory of Her

poems by
Matt Amott

Dedicated to the Summer crush...
that lasts all year long.

Her postcard

arrives, unsigned.
She writes
of road trips, lust
and Wilson Pickett.

My roommates know
it's for me.

Insomniac

Just off a twelve hour shift
on a crappy Monday
and the car won't start,
he walks home
with heavy steps.

He passes the bar
with dollar drafts
and a tied ball game,
but he's not interested
tonight.

Six hours
before his next shift
he longs for sleep,

he's not even through the door
before he drops everything,
a trail of clothes
follow him
to his bed.
He eases
under the sheets,
alarm set
lights out.

The phone rings,
it's her.

"I can't sleep"
she says
"can you talk for a bit?"

"Sure"
he says
"I wasn't tired
anyway."

Summer Crush

She stands on the edge
of the pool,
an all American girl in her
red, white and blue bikini.
She looks my way
and gives me a smile
before she leaps
through the warm July air
and is engulfed
by refreshing waters.

Totally cool.

And I'm left sitting
on the hot patio as she
swims away,
while a bead of sweat
trickles down my face.
Probably from the heat,
but I can't say for sure.

Drinks With Hank

My dinner date cancelled last minute,
leaving me a quiet evening
to have some drinks and
listen to Bukowski
reading poems on the hi-fi.

I log onto Facebook
to see the latest photos
from a tattoo artist
I know.
Ventricles and valves
of a crimson heart
being tattooed on
a well endowed
breast.

In the background,
Bukowski reads
about someone else
getting action
tonight.

Get Well Soon

The cute bartender
serving us drinks
overheard our break up
the last time
we were at Harry's.

So when I returned alone
a few days later,
she brought over
a shot of whiskey
and said
"this is for the wound…"
then slipped me her number
on a matchbook
"…and this is for
a speedy recovery."

Winter Solstice

The longest night.
More time
to ramble
and laugh,
more time
for another bottle,
another smoke,
and to sit in the bed
of the truck
holding your hand
a little longer
while the stars
slow down
to watch
our smiles.

So Long

On my last night
in town, the bar

is full of past
loves, hook-ups
and train wrecks.
I stay
until last call
for a final round,
a final dance,
and the hope
for a final kiss.

With my belongings packed
and a hangover,
I leave early
with an open road
ahead.

The radio up to ten
while my hazy memory
sorts through
the ones who
said they'll come
visit
and those
who just said
goodbye.

Judging a Book By It's Cover

I can't keep the books
of my favorite writers.
I read them too much.
Thrown into backpacks
and stuffed into pockets
with broken edges
and dog-eared pages
until they simply fall apart.

On our first date,
she said she had
a love for poetry.
But then I saw
her collection of books,
all shiny and pristine.
Upon hearing
the spines crack
when opened,
I knew it wasn't
going to work out.

Blood Moon

She and I
climb the hill
to watch
the Lunar eclipse.
Upon the blanket,
empty bottles
swept aside.
Kisses so deep,
we barely notice
the moon
blushing
above.

The Sundress

As she
walks away,
the bottom
of her dress
sweeps across
the back of her thighs
like a palm tree swaying
in a tropical breeze.
Later that night
I order rum
and think of the trees,
hoping the breeze
blows her back
my way.

The Silent Treatment

Staying a few days
at a friend's place,
he showed me
his latest
technological purchase.
It was a little machine
that looks like
a hockey puck.
It plays music,
answers random questions,
tells you the weather,
news and trivia
just by saying
her name.
While my friend was away at work
I asked her to play some music,
Black Sabbath, MC5,
Muddy Waters, anything.
I got nothing.
The weather,
nothing.
Some trivia,
still nothing.
This went on all day.

When my friend returned,
I told him
his machine was broken.

I say,
all day long
I've been trying
to get her to work,

play songs,
give a fun fact,
I even spoke
sweetly to her.
Angie, please
tell me the weather.

He laughed
and corrected me,
"Her name is Alexa."

It wasn't
the first time
I got the silent treatment
in search of companionship.

Valentine's Day

Perfect placement,
in the midst
of the snowy season,

the heat
from your lips,
warms my blood
of winter's chill.

Take This Call

Only the crazies
would scream
down the city
streets.

Now Bluetooth
makes us all
look fucking
nuts.

Heart Condition

The doctors don't like the prognosis,
they say my heart rate is too high
and my blood pressure is reaching critical.
But I can tell you right now,
it's not the cheeseburgers or Po'Boys,
nor is it the beer I wash them down with.

It's her.

The way
she enters
a room,
her voice,
the talk,
and the walk,
her eyes,
the curve of her neck,
her smarts
and her sass.
We are arm in arm
out and about
during the day
and wrapped around
each other
under the sheets
at night.

She gets the blood racing
and my heart kicks into
high gear just to keep up.
When it finally explodes
I hope
she

is listed
as cause of death.

Travelers

Everything turns up a notch
when we both arrive
in the same city.
Marrow eaters,
sucking the life,
until the keg is tapped out
and the band goes home.

Both reckless,
storming the streets
as champions.
He clears a path
through the heathens
of Saturday night
and I linger
a few feet behind.
Watching the mad one
burn like Kerouac,
I am Sal
to his Dean Moriarty.
Reporting the antics
to the masses,
pen in one hand
and camera in the other
because mere words
won't do.

There has to be proof
of all these events
or I will be labeled
a writer of fiction.

To Ride Eternal
for Annie Menebroker

Years ago,
she commented
on some
train photos
I took.

"Still a
railroad man
I see."

"Always!"

"Good! It makes me
happy to know you're
out there somewhere."

I thought the same
last night,
when I heard
she passed
and was finally
pain free.

Happy to know
she's out there too—
somewhere.

Zig Zag Falls

Snow blocked the road
to the top of the mountain,
so we backtracked
a bit to Zig Zag.
Charging
up the trail
through the powder.
She tightly
held my hand
until we reached
the end.
The normally raging
falls were quiet
in the cold.
Frozen still
as if the
waters stopped,
not wanting
to disturb our
first kiss.

Strongly Worded Letter

He sits alone at a bar
next to an empty chair
that was supposed to be
for her.

A bottle of Old Crow
sits between two glasses,
one empty
and one emptied
many times.

He rereads the letter
that said she wasn't coming,

something about
if it's too good
to be true,
it probably is.

He pulls out a wad of cash
and lays it on the bar

asking the barkeep
for something
from the top shelf.

The barkeep asks,
"You need something stronger?"

Yeah,
the Crow alone
can't carry away
the memory of her.

A Poem With No Words

We walk
through the streets
side by side
laughing
while in my mind
I am searching
for a poem
but I am failing.

A verse,
a line
anything
to express
the exquisite beauty
I see
in your smile.

Not Shelley
nor Bryon
nor Neruda
have the words,

but the poetry lies
only in my silence

as the breath
escapes me

when you reach
for my hand.

Lonesome Whistle

The sound
of the whistle
travels farther
on cold nights
reaching more
broken
hearts wishing
that train
would take
them far
away from
any thoughts
of her.

Playing the Field

I usually stay away
from sports bars,
too many big screens
too many team jerseys
and too many high fives.
But, my day was long
and Mulligan's is
the closest place
to get myself a few drinks.

When I arrive,
there is an attractive woman
sitting at the bar.
She seems to be with a group
but not with anyone in particular
and when we hold
each other's gaze
a little longer
than usual,
I walk
towards her
preparing
for tonight's game.

Every Cloud

I remember the click
of your heels
on the hardwood floor
that morning you left.

Now when it rains,
the ceiling leaks and
dripping water reminds me
of the sound of you leaving.
Although, it could also be
the sound of you
coming back.

Fallen

My friend proposed
to his girlfriend
in San Francisco.

They were on a boat
under the Golden Gate bridge,
where hundreds have leapt
into the frigid unknown abyss.

As so did he.

A Chill In the Air

The sound of her
yelling at me
was momentarily
drowned out
by noisy geese
overhead
flying South
for the winter,
but her
icy gaze
held.

And that's when
I left.
Following the birds
to a warmer climate.

Grazing

I read
her books
at night,
when
I'm wanting
and alone.
Her seductive words,
so fearless,
jump
from the page
and wrap themselves
around my head,
just where
I want her
legs
to be.

In The Pines

After one of our
brutal arguments,
I spend the entire evening
walking around the city
reflecting on all
the hell
we've been through
the last few years.

When I return back
to the apartment
in the morning,
she asks
"Where did you sleep last night?"
I know she expects to hear
that I went to a bar,
got drunk and went home
with some random woman
but I say nothing
and go to bed thinking
if things keep going
this way
she just may get
the answer
she's looking for.

Subject to Interpretation

I was asked to read
with other poets at a book release.
Getting there early I discovered
I was reading last,
but it was happy hour
and beers were only a buck.
Me and some friends grabbed
a table and listened to the other poets
while the waitress kept my tab running.

After an hour it was my turn,
I leapt to the stage and gave the performance of a
lifetime.
I read like a champion.
Poems flowed with hand gesture and feeling.
The crowd roared
and begged for more.
After my last line,
the room erupted,
a standing ovation
my friends hoisted
me on their shoulders
and carried me
into the streets.

A friend called
the next day,
told me that I was lucky I wasn't arrested!
He said,
after drinking twelve bottles of Budweiser,
they called my name.
I barely made it up
to the stage and when I did,

I swore, slurred and waved my arms like a
madman,
throwing insults at the audience
if they didn't clap
fast enough.
When the crowd demanded
I abandon the stage,
I challenged them all
to a fist fight,
"just like Hemingway would."

When I was done, I stumbled
over chairs and people,
stopped only
to yell one last insult,
bowed
to the twelve empty bottles
that stood tall
on our table
before they grabbed me
and whisked me out of there.

As I took in
all this new information
I thought to myself,

twelve empty bottles?

So there was a standing ovation.

Departure

I watch
as your plane takes off
higher and higher and higher
until you are gone.
Wishing it was me
who made you feel
like you were lost
in the clouds.

Classic Country

When I first saw her
she was putting quarters
in the jukebox.
When she came back to the bar
I asked what she picked.
It was country,
but she said she
didn't like the classics
only the new Nashville,
CMT, pop country.

We only dated
a few months before
I broke it off.
She was good
but she wasn't
a classic.

Bukowski's Heaven

Sitting at Phillipe's
with a French dip
and *Run With the Hunted*
when in walks
a woman,

long legs
in a short skirt.
High heels tighten
every muscle
under smooth,
tan skin.
Then I remember
your perversion,

your womanizing ways
and now,
women from your past
visit
to scold you.
Walking
over your grave
in short skirts.
And you,

you just lay there
six feet under
smiling
looking up
into their
pearly gates.

Desired Destination

The message
on the machine
was clear.

She ran into
an old flame
while on the trip,
her first true love.
What are the odds?

I promised to pick her up
at the train station,
watched them kiss
on the platform.

Nearby
a mighty
Santa Fe
grinds
to a halt
while
my heartbreak
rumbles on,
knowing
I am not
her
desired
destination.

A New Tune

Every morning
the bird
outside my window
sings early,

much to my dismay.

But now
I wake
next to you
and finally understand
his song.

The Golden Age

Watching a classic,
the blonde bombshell
on the movie screen
looks
at the man
with smoldering eyes
and in her sultry voice
tells him
if he needs her
"Just put your lips
together and blow."

I walked home
from the movie theater
whistling the whole way
and when no one came
I thought,
they sure don't make 'em
like that anymore.

Unwelcome Inspiration

Two poets sit in a bar
on a warm summer day
having a few drinks
and catching up.

One poet says,
"Did you hear that
Matt's wife took off
on him?"

"I didn't!"
said the other,
"that's horrible."

"It sure is"
continued the poet,
"she quit her job
and refused to get another
while she went through all
their savings.
Then she started
messing around
with other guys
and left him
with no money
only a dear John letter."

"Tragic!"
said the other poet,
"having to deal
with that kind of
heartbreak,
loneliness

and pain."

They sipped
their beers quietly
until one finally admitted,
"That lucky bastard
will probably have
a new book of poems
out by Christmas."

Matt Amott is a poet, musician and photographer who rambles around the Pacific Northwest. He is co-founder and co-editor of Six Ft. Swells Press and has been published in numerous collections as well as two books of his own, *The Coast is Clear* (Six Ft. Swells Press) and *Get Well Soon* (Epic Rites Press). He can be reached and purchases made at www.sixftswellspress.com.

www.ingramcontent.com/pod-product-compliance
Lightning Source LLC
Chambersburg PA
CBHW022343040426
42449CB00006B/702